UP CLOSE ™

PIRATES

PAUL HARRISON

PowerKIDS
press

New York

Published in 2008 by The Rosen Publishing Group, Inc.
29 East 21st Street, New York, NY 10010

Author: Paul Harrison
Editor (new edition): Kate Overy
Designer (new edition): Sylvie Rabbe
Editor (US edition): Kara Murray

Picture credits: Bridgeman Art Library: page 16, bottom left; Corbis: front cover; page 5; page 19, top and bottom right; Chris Collingwood: page 14; Indy Magnoli: page 21, bottom right; Kobal Collection: page 2, page 7, bottom right, page 8, page 9, top and bottom right, page 12, bottom left, page 13, top and bottom, page 15, top and middle, page 20, top right, page 21, top right; Mary Evans: page 7, top left, page 20, bottom left; Reuters: page 18, bottom left; The Art Archive: page 12, middle right, page 24; Topfoto: page 10, bottom, page 11, bottom right, page 15, bottom right.

Library of Congress Cataloging-in-Publication Data

Harrison, Paul, 1969–
    Pirates / Paul Harrison.
        p. cm. — (Up close)
    Includes index.
    ISBN 978-1-4042-4226-5 (lib. bdg.)
    1. Pirates—Juvenile literature. I. Title. II. Series.

    G535.H325 2008
    910.4'5—dc22

                                        2007033503

Manufactured in China

CONTENTS

Who Were the

Pirates have been sailing the high seas and plundering towns and ships for centuries. The golden age of piracy was during the 1700s when famous pirates ruled the Caribbean waters. But where did the cutthroat business of piracy start? Who were the pirates?

VIKING WEAPONS

The Vikings liked their weapons. Their most deadly was the double-edged lightweight sword, which measured almost 36 inches (91 cm)! But only very successful Vikings could afford such weaponry; most made do with short swords, spears, and broad axes. One of their greatest weapons was the longship, which was very light and designed to move quickly through water. This made carrying out raids much easier.

SCANDINAVIAN SCARERS

For 300 years much of Northern Europe was terrorized by raiders from Scandinavia, the Vikings. From the eighth century A.D. on, these fearless warriors would plunder and steal before heading home with their ill-gotten gains. The Vikings also settled and traded in much of Europe and traveled as far as Istanbul, but it was their habit of pillaging and fighting that built their reputation.

Pirates?

GOLDEN YEARS

The so-called "golden age" of piracy lasted from the late 1600s to the early 1700s. This is when many famous pirates were active in the Caribbean. However, before this golden age, piracy was the preserve of the buccaneers—originally a bunch of mixed but mainly French hunters. By the mid-1600s the Spanish, who had claimed much of the Caribbean, tried to get rid of these lawless hunters, but the buccaneers fought back, plundering Spanish ships and raiding towns, which was probably more profitable than hunting wild pigs.

DRESSED TO KILL

Vikings didn't wear uniforms unless they were specially chosen to fight for the king's army. Most Vikings didn't wear much in the way of armor because they needed to be light on their feet, although some wore helmets. Well-off Vikings sometimes wore a sheet of chain mail known as a byrnie, but an average Viking wore a tunic that hung below the waist, a leather jacket, woolen socks, and calfskin boots.

Legal Piracy

When is a pirate not a pirate? The answer is when he is a privateer—a sailor given permission to act like a pirate. So how and when might this be the case, and why would anyone want to legalize piracy?

CORSAIRS

Not all pirates came from the Caribbean. The seas around North Africa were plagued by pirates known as the corsairs. The corsairs, or Barbary pirates as they were also known, used to capture prisoners to hold for ransom or to sell as slaves. The most famous corsairs were the Barbarossa brothers who operated out of Algiers during the early 1500s.

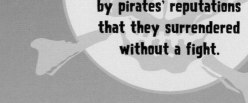

In a lot of cases, pirates wouldn't even have to fire a shot! Ships' captains were so frightened by pirates' reputations that they surrendered without a fight.

A LETTER OF MARQUE

When some European nations were at war, they would issue the captains of ships with what was called a letter of marque, a permit from the king or queen that allowed them to steal cargoes and ships from the enemy. All the captains had to do was split their booty with the king or queen. Some captains kept it up even when their country was no longer at war. With no letter of marque they were simply pirates. It did mean they could keep all the treasure to themselves, though. One of the most famous privateers was Sir Francis Drake. (See his statue, left.)

DAILY RISKS

Being a pirate was by definition a dangerous job. People fighting and firing shots at each other—not to mention the day-to-day dangers of sailing, such as falling off masts or being hit by flying rigging—meant that there were an awful lot of disfigured sailors out there. Badly injured sailors often worked as ships' cooks. I wonder if any missing limbs ended up in the cooking pot?

THE BACKLASH

Without the state seal of approval, pirating could be a very risky business. Governments and law enforcers showed little mercy toward those they captured. If captured, people suspected of piracy faced trial for their crimes and the toughest of penalties. Most trials lasted two days, and almost all resulted in execution. Their executions were often really gory and happened in public places to discourage people from a life of piracy.

Myth vs. Reality

Everyone knows something about pirates, whether it's what they were supposed to have looked like or what they got up to. However, not everything you might have heard is true. How much of what you know is accurate—and how much is just plain wrong?

WHO'S A PRETTY BOY THEN?

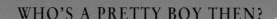

According to the movies, no pirate would be complete without a parrot. Unlikely though this may sound, it does have some basis in reality. Pirates with cash to offload often bought themselves pets that they could take aboard the ship with them. Parrots were popular since they could be taught to speak, which gave pirates something to do during quiet periods. More popular still were monkeys, but basically anything small and entertaining was welcome.

8

DIVING BOARD

One of the most famous of dastardly pirate deeds was making captives walk the plank—forcing them along a board that stuck out from the boat until they fell into the often shark-infested waters. Guess what? There's no evidence that this ever really happened. For a start, it seems like an awful lot of effort to go to. If they wanted to get rid of a captive they'd probably just have chucked him overboard. That would be much simpler.

LAW-ABIDING CITIZENS?

Despite being lawless thieves in the eyes of most people, many pirates actually lived by a set of strict rules called the pirate code. The code varied from ship to ship but generally followed similar lines. Pirates voted on where the ship would go and agreed on how treasure would be shared. The code also covered health and safety, with regulations against leaving lights unattended, fighting among the crew, and not maintaining weapons. Unbelievably there were sometimes rules that forbade gambling. Not what you would expect, is it?

Pirates didn't bury treasure, which also means they didn't have treasure maps.

Pirate Essentials

So what did you need to be a pirate during the golden age of piracy? Well, there were a number of things that no self-respecting buccaneer could do without.

GET THE POINT

Pirates used any kind of weapon they could get their hands on, including clubs and axes. If it could do someone some harm then it was good enough. One of the most common weapons were short, sharp swords. The beauty of such a weapon was that it didn't take a great deal of skill to use and its short blade made it ideal for fighting on the cramped decks of boats.

BANG BANG

One pirate favorite was the flintlock pistol, which got its name because it used a piece of flint to light the gunpowder to fire the shot. It was light and easily available but it wasn't the perfect weapon. It fired only one lead ball at a time and had to be reloaded after every shot. Also, flintlocks often failed to fire at all—especially if the gunpowder got wet. That's why pirates like Blackbeard often carried more than one pistol when going into battle.

Many people think that a pirate's sword was called a cutlass—in fact, that particular type of short sword wasn't common until after the golden age of piracy.

SOMEWHERE TO CALL HOME

Pirates didn't spend all their time on board their boats, of course—they needed somewhere to spend all their ill-gotten gains. Towns like Port Royal in Jamaica and the island of New Providence became pirate hideaways. These hideouts were never the safest places to stay—they were full of thieving, murdering pirates, for one thing. Occasionally, mother nature got in on the act, too. In 1692 a tidal wave swept away most of Port Royal, taking many of its inhabitants with it.

SHIVER ME TIMBERS

You're not a pirate if you don't have a boat—otherwise you're just a thief. Although some pirates used large, heavily armed boats, most pirates preferred small quick boats known as sloops. These single-masted ships didn't need a large crew to sail them, which meant that any treasure they stole didn't have to be shared between very many people. Also, fast sloops were excellent at quickly getting away from any warships that might be on the prowl.

Treasure

People became pirates for lots of different reasons. They might have been running away from a crime they had committed elsewhere; perhaps they were part of a crew that had been overtaken by pirates and they decided to join them; or maybe they just liked the life. No matter how they got to be pirates they were all joined by one aim—to get as rich as possible!

BITS AND PIECES

The main currency of the time was Spanish, and the most important coins were the gold doubloon and the silver peso, or dollar as it was sometimes known. The peso was more famously called a piece of eight. This was because it was worth eight reales—a lower value Spanish coin. Sometimes the dollars were actually cut into pieces, which sounds like a pretty drastic way of getting some loose change.

BURIED TREASURE

Despite what you might have heard, pirates really didn't bury treasure. The idea came from a rumor that a pirate called Captain Kidd buried his treasure on some remote island. In reality pirates never held on to their ill-gotten gains long enough to bury them. No sooner had they set foot on land, they had spent it all on liquor, women, and gambling. Often the pirates would spend the equivalent of a lifetime's wages in a matter of weeks. That's not exactly what you call saving for the future.

BLACK BART

Possibly the most successful pirate of all time was Bartholomew Roberts. During his piratical career, "Black Bart," as he was known, raided ships on both sides of the Atlantic. In one raid alone he captured a Portuguese ship and took over 90,000 gold coins called moidores, many priceless jewels, as well as the boat's valuable cargo. Roberts didn't get to enjoy his wealth for long—he died in a battle in 1722 after just three years of pirating.

An amnesty in 1717 said that pirates would be spared trial if they promised to give up their pirating ways. They could keep their treasure, too!

SNEAKY PIRATES

One of the sneakiest pirate raids took place in 1716 when around 300 pirates led by Henry Jennings raided a Spanish camp on the east coast of America. The Spanish had been recovering silver pesos that had been lost when their fleet of treasure ships had sunk in a storm. Jennings' raid was a great success and the pirate fleet made off with around 350,000 pieces of eight—an absolute fortune! How annoyed must the Spanish have been? They lost their treasure in the storm, found it, and then lost it again.

13

Famous Pirates

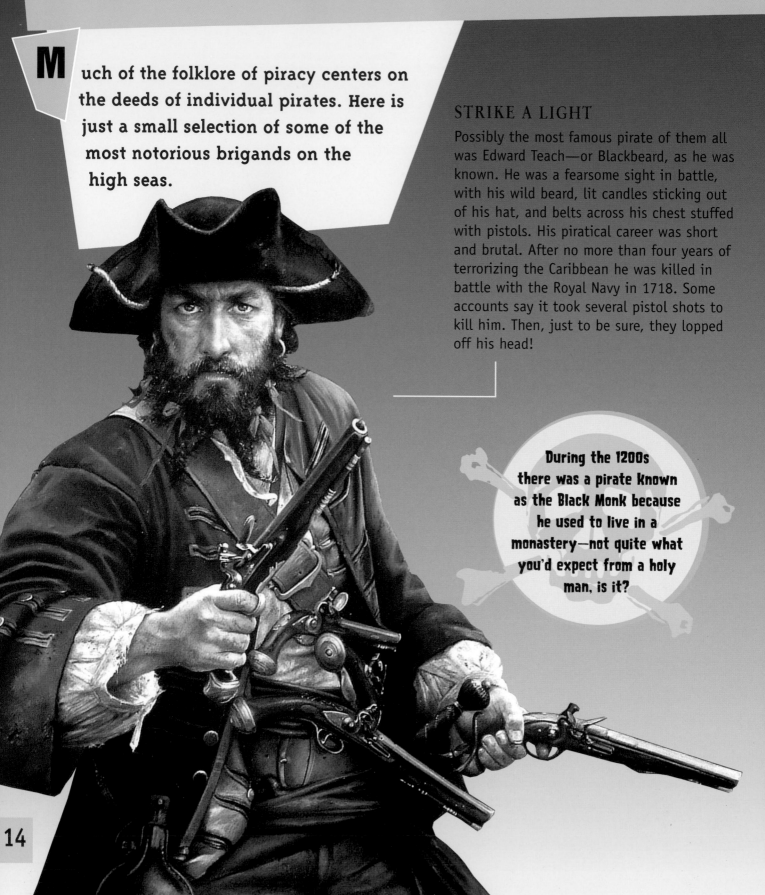

Much of the folklore of piracy centers on the deeds of individual pirates. Here is just a small selection of some of the most notorious brigands on the high seas.

STRIKE A LIGHT

Possibly the most famous pirate of them all was Edward Teach—or Blackbeard, as he was known. He was a fearsome sight in battle, with his wild beard, lit candles sticking out of his hat, and belts across his chest stuffed with pistols. His piratical career was short and brutal. After no more than four years of terrorizing the Caribbean he was killed in battle with the Royal Navy in 1718. Some accounts say it took several pistol shots to kill him. Then, just to be sure, they lopped off his head!

During the 1200s there was a pirate known as the Black Monk because he used to live in a monastery—not quite what you'd expect from a holy man, is it?

ANYTHING YOU CAN DO

Pirates were, by and large, men; though there were some exceptions to the rule. Mary Read and Anne Bonny were two of the most famous female pirates. They sailed with Jack "Calico" Rackham, another well-known pirate, but their combined talents didn't stop them from being captured in 1720. The usual punishment for people found guilty of being pirates was hanging. Both Mary Read and Anne Bonny escaped the hangman's noose because they were both pregnant.

HAVE A HEART

Possibly the most bloodthirsty of all the pirates was Francois L'Ollonais, who gained a deserved reputation for torturing and murdering his prisoners in gruesome ways—one time he even ate the heart of one of his captives. In 1668 his greed got the better of him and he went on one raid too many. He and his crew were ambushed by some Native Americans and L'Ollonais was killed. Some reports even suggest that he was eaten—perhaps unlikely, but he would have deserved it!

RUM FELLOW

One of the most successful pirates was Captain Henry Morgan, who is so famous there's a rum named after him. He was really a privateer, though some of his raids happened after a treaty had been signed between England and Spain. Morgan claimed to have no knowledge of the treaty, so he got away with his piracy. He managed to do what few pirates ever did— retire rich. He was also knighted and made Lieutenant Governor of Jamaica. And they say that crime doesn't pay.

Battles on the

Gold doesn't come cheap, and pirates had to fight tooth and nail to earn their wage. There were some ferocious battles on the high seas, and only the toughest survived.

DARK LEGEND

Samuel Bellamy's pirate career lasted under a year, but he certainly made an impression! Bellamy was known as Black Sam and was a close associate of the infamous Blackbeard. Over the course of that year he captured more than 50 ships before he was killed at age 29. His most famous raid was in 1717, when he and his crew chased down and captured a 300 ton (272 t) slave ship called the *Whydah Gally*.

CROSS OF THE DUTCHMEN

Pier Gerlofs Donia, a famous Dutch pirate, was renowned for his size and strength. He also commanded a fearsome crew. In 1515, they captured no fewer than 28 Dutch ships, and Pier became known as the Cross of the Dutchmen. But even this wasn't enough for Pier, as he went on to ransack the towns of Medemblik and Alkmarr, in Holland.

16

Sea

OPPORTUNISTS

Pirates had to make sure that they had the perfect ship for battle. It had to be light, easy to maneuver, and stocked with weapons! Remember, pirates couldn't build a ship to order like the military did, so they had to make do with odds and ends from the ships they looted. Sometimes, they would steal an entire ship!

Pirates didn't just steal gold and silver—they also stole things that they could use, such as food, alcohol, medicine, and clothes.

BIG GUNS

Of course, a captain had to have a crew, and this would include the first mate, a cook, a surgeon, and probably a carpenter. The gunner was also an important member of the crew. Gunners would lead their own separate group of four to six men in charge of artillery. The gunner himself would aim the cannon while his men would be in charge of loading, firing, and resetting. All those men for one cannon!

Dangerous

Although the golden age of piracy finished nearly 300 years ago, it didn't spell the end of piracy completely. While the world still contains thieves and boats, there will always be pirates; and that's as true today as it was all those years ago.

HOSED OFF

Pirate attacks are known to happen in Asian waters. One pirate crew off the coast of Malaysia chased a Japanese cargo vessel for three-quarters of an hour. The brave crew of the cargo vessel refused to be boarded, though, and despite the fact that the pirates were armed, the Japanese fought them off. And what weapons did the Japanese crew use? They used high-pressure hoses. Those pirates must have had one damp voyage home. How humiliating.

HUNTED DOWN

Malaysia, Singapore, and Indonesia, which all border the notorious pirate haunt of the Malacca Straits, have combined to fight modern-day pirates. Now a fleet of 17 ships patrols the straits, which is one of the busiest shipping lanes in the world. They can even call on air force backup if needed. The Chinese navy is also very active in hunting down pirate crews.

Although piracy still goes on, your chances of ever meeting a pirate are incredibly remote.

Waters

MODERN MENACE

Somalia, a country on the east coast of Africa, has a growing problem with piracy. As with most countries with a piracy problem, it is poor and has suffered from an unstable government and famine. The Somalian pirates generally attack cargo vessels, which they aim to hijack to sell the goods on the black market.

NEW WEAPONS

Instead of sloops, today's pirates use small motorboats—handy for speedy attacks and dodging through shallow waters where bigger boats can't chase them. Instead of flintlock pistols and swords, some use machine guns and rocket launchers. However, most modern-day pirates are poorly equipped and some still chase boats with little more than clubs and machetes, which are cutlasslike knives—pretty much like the pirates of the golden age.

Entertaining

Most people form their image of pirates from different sources but usually not the history books. Instead, the pictures we have in our heads come from countless films, stories, and paintings. It's great entertainment, but is it accurate? The answer is no, it generally isn't.

JOHNNY BOY

The most popular pirate of today is without a doubt Johnny Depp's character from the *Pirates of the Caribbean* films, Captain Jack Sparrow. He is witty, charming and good looking—exactly the opposite of most real pirates. He also gets to fight with pirates who have come back from the grave, which real pirates didn't do, obviously. Then again, the movies were never claiming to be an accurate portrayal of pirate life, and they are really fun to watch.

REAL WRITING

One book that was believed to be fiction has turned out, or so many people think, to be true after all. It's called *A General History of the Robbings and Murders of the Most Notorious Pirates*, which isn't the snappiest title you're likely to come across. Its author is a Captain Charles Johnson, but it was believed to have been written by Daniel Defoe, the author of *Robinson Crusoe*, among other books. The book tells the life stories of a number of different pirates. Since it was written so close to the golden age of piracy it is an invaluable source for historians. It's also a great read.

Pirates

Most of the classic drawings you see of pirates are by the Victorian illustrators Howard Pyle and N. C. Wyeth.

THE CLASSIC

The classic pirate is, of course, Long John Silver from the book *Treasure Island*, by Robert Louis Stevenson. In this book, not only does Silver have a peg leg and a parrot called Captain Flint, he's also after some buried treasure, marked on a map by a big cross. This book, more than any other, has contributed to the public's idea of what a pirate should look like.

BUCCANEERING BALLADS

During the Victorian period the image of the pirate became more romanticized. In 1879 Gilbert and Sullivan wrote a comic opera called *The Pirates of Penzance*, which featured a less-than-bloodthirsty crew of pirates. The pirates were from Penzance in Cornwall, England, which was hardly a hive of piratical activity.

Glossary

AMBUSH (AM-bush)
Waiting or hiding from people before attacking them.

ARTILLERY (ahr-TIH-lur-ee)
A mounted weapon, usually a gun or cannon.

BUCCANEER (buh-kuh-NEER)
A pirate who preyed on ships in the Caribbean in the seventeenth and eighteenth centuries.

DOUBLOON (duh-BLOON)
A gold coin once used as currency in Spain and Spanish America.

FINTLOCK (FLINT-lok)
A weapon in which a piece of flint is used to ignite a spark.

LAWLESS (LAH-less)
Operating outside of the law.

MACHETE (muh-SHEH-tee)
A broad knife often used as a weapon.

MANEUVER (muh-NOO-ver)
A complicated, skillful movement, usually preplanned.

MONASTERY (MAHN-uh-ster-ee)
A building used to house religious communities, usually monks.

NOTORIOUS (no-TOR-ee-us)
Famous for bad deeds.

PRIVATEER (pry-vuh-TEER)
A person or people employed by the government to attack or harass enemy ships.

RAID (RAYD)
A sudden attack or assault, often resulting in theft.

REGULATION (reh-gyuh-LAY-shun)
A law or set of rules.

RIGGING (RIG-ing)
An apparatus attached to the hull of a ship in order to make the boat move as a whole. It includes cordage, sails, and masts.

Further Reading

PIRATES

by John Matthews
New York: Atheneum Books for Young Readers, 2006

THE HISTORY OF PIRATES

by Angus Konstam
Guilford, CT: The Lyons Press, 2002

PIRATE (DK EYEWITNESS BOOKS)

by Richard Platt
New York: Dorling Kindersley, 2004

THE BEST BOOK OF PIRATES

by Barnaby Howard
Boston: Kingfisher, 2006

CARIBBEAN PIRATES: A TREASURE CHEST OF FACT, FICTION AND FOLKLORE

by George Beahm
Charlottesville, VA: Hampton Roads Publishing Company, Inc., 2007

THE BOOK OF PIRATES

by Howard Pyle
Mineola, NY: Dover Publications, 2007

WEB SITES

Due to the changing nature of Internet links, PowerKids Press has developed an online list of Web sites related to the subject of this book. This site is updated regularly. Please use this link to access the list: www.powerkidslinks.com/upcl/pirates/

Index